Writing as a Tool for Self-Discovery

Writing as a Tool for Self-Discovery

Heather Hughes-Calero

COASTLINE PUBLISHING COMPANY
1988

In service to the SUGMAD

Cover and text design by Lois Stanfield

Coastline Publishing Company
P.O. Box 223062
Carmel, California 93922
(408) 625-9388

Printed in the United States of America
First Edition

Library of Congress Catalog No.: 87-073482
ISBN: 0-932927-06-8

**To Hank, who needled me into writing this book,
and to writers everywhere.**

Contents

ABOUT THE AUTHOR   13

CHAPTER 1

The Great Secret of Writing   15

Exercise 1 Awareness Technique   24

CHAPTER 2

Probing the Imagination   35

Exercise 2 Daydreaming a Scene   49
Exercise 3 Photograph Technique   50

CHAPTER 3

Breaking the Writers Block/Working with Patterns   55

Exercise 4 Using Patterns   61

CHAPTER 4

Viewpoint/Attitude/Attention   73

Exercise 5 Patterns for Viewpoint   81

Exercise 6 Viewpoint Studies: Still Life 88

Exercise 7 Viewpoint Studies: Looking Glass Technique 90

Exercise 8 Viewpoint Studies: Conversation 92

Exercise 9 Viewpoint Studies: Public Library Technique 94

C H A P T E R 5

The Creative Process/The Winning Writer's Consciousness

97

Exercise 10 Making the Invisible Visible 107

Exercise 11 Finding the Inner Voice 108

C H A P T E R 6

Developing Inner Sight/Tapping Into the Creative Flow 111

Exercise 12 Developing Soft Vision: Paper Technique 120

Exercise 13 Developing Peripheral Senses: Walking Technique 122

Exercise 14 Writing from Your Peripheral Senses 124

C O N C L U S I O N

125

About the Author

Heather Hughes-Calero is the author of five novels—*The Sedona Trilogy:* Book 1 *Through The Crystal* (March, 1985); Book 2 *Doorways Between The Worlds* (July, 1985); Book 3 *The Land of Nome* (November, 1985); *The Golden Dream* (September 1987); and *The Secrets of Arhirit*, which was written in 1986 but has not yet been released. *Writing As A Tool For Self-Discovery* is her first non-fiction book, although she has written numerous articles for national magazines.

Following the success of *The Sedona Trilogy*, Mrs. Hughes-Calero began teaching writing as a tool for self-discovery and has inspired writers by conducting special workshops throughout the United States. For the past three years she has taught a course on the same subject in the community services division at Monterey Peninsula College.

Mrs. Hughes-Calero has also enjoyed a successful career in broadcasting. Earlier she taught high school English and creative writing. At one point in her life, she spent a year in Japan, living in Buddhist temples while working with translators on an ancient Sanskrit text.

The author lives with her husband, her two dogs, a cat, and a horse on a small California ranch. She is an ECK initiate.

CHAPTER 1

The Great Secret of Writing

* Are you a professional writer but feel yourself getting a bit stale in your work?

* Do you want to be a professional but can't seem to generate the motivation to succeed? Is your life too busy? Are you always planning to write when things quiet down?

* Do you have a monkey on your back-that is, is there always that feeling that something is sitting on your shoulder urging you to write? Deep down are you afraid-afraid you can't do it or, worse, afraid that people you care about will poke fun if you do?

* Are you interested in writing, not for publication, but for the sheer joy of communicating your thoughts through words?

* Do you want to perfect a style of letter or memo writing, purely for the sake of being understood, to communicate not what someone thought you said, but what you did say?

* Do you want to enrich your writing as a tool for self-discovery?

Down with Fear

A few years ago, I went backpacking alone with my two small dogs in the wilderness area above Oak Creek Canyon of Arizona. We had hiked a rugged eight miles up to an elevation of 7,500 feet. There we found a beautiful sandy beach next to a fast-running stream. The spot was no more than fifteen feet wide, pushed up against a towering Ponderosa forest.

It was almost sunset when we arrived so I quickly set up camp and made a fire, then fed both myself and the dogs. We didn't have much time before darkness settled into the forest and so it wasn't long before I was nestled into my sleeping bag gazing up at the stars, the dogs sleeping contentedly on the ground next to me.

Suddenly, lying there, I heard something coming toward us. My ear close to the ground, I listened ... *Crunch* ... *Crunch* ... *Crunch*. Leaves were crackling and branches seemed to be snapping under the foot of some giant beast. My heart began to pound. Thinking that it might be a bear, I quickly leashed my two small dogs, held them tightly to me in one arm and grabbed for the flashlight with the other. Just as the footfalls of the beast came alongside us, I turned on the light. To my surprise, I came eye to eye not with a bear but a fieldmouse. The mouse took one look at me and ran off in a fit of terror. I burst out laughing. I was laughing at myself, because what I had imagined to be so large and terrible was only a beast that was merely two inches high. To the writer, the imagined beast of the written word is only a small foe making a large noise.

There Is A Great Secret To Writing (and to living life).

Do you dream in color?

Do you daydream in color?

Dreaming and daydreaming in color are sure signs of a creative imagination. It is a plus factor for anyone who wishes to succeed in any artistic field. The dreamer or the daydreamer has already developed his or her creative nature to some extent, to the extent of seeing vividly in living color. For those who do not dream in color, the ability to do so can be developed. Simply remind yourself to notice color in your everyday activities. When you sit down and gaze out the window and begin to daydream, catch yourself in the act and remind yourself to look at the colors in the scene of your imagination. As you practice in this way, you will be establishing a habit in your consciousness. Very soon color will be an automatic part of your daydream and will spill over into your nightdreams as well.

What Are Your Daydreams Like?

Now it is time to ask yourself what your daydreams are like. What do they tell you? Do you see yourself as a successful writer or do you see yourself as mediocre, or even as someone who'd like to write but is afraid to try?

If you want to write, if you want to be successful, you have to train yourself to actually see yourself fulfilling your desires. Talking to yourself about success and other affirmations won't help a bit if, in your imagination, your daydreams, you see yourself as a failure. It may take a bit of effort but you can train yourself to daydream positively. The key here is to *Improve Your Daydreams. Develop Them. Your Writing Will Improve* (and so will everything else in your life). This is a part of the great secret of writing. In truth, *Your Image Pattern, or Daydreaming Pattern, is Reflected in The Life You Live.*

Let's step away from the secret we are approaching. We are getting close to it but we are not yet ready to examine it. There are some ground rules to be set down first.

The Mechanical Side of Writing

Everything in life has a mechanical side to it. There are basic rules that must be accepted before a successful venture can take place. For the writer, the mechanics are broken down into four basic rules.

Rule 1. Grammar, Spelling, Punctuation, and Sentence Construction

There is no getting away from it. If you are going to write in a particular language, you must know the mechanics of that language. Once you have mastered them, you can make changes to suit the personality of your writing style and still be clearly understood. This is often the case with fiction.

Rule 2. Self-Discipline

Julie Andrews once said, "Some people regard discipline as a chore. For me, it is a kind of order that sets me free to fly."

Self-discipline is an all-important ingredient to success in any field but to the writer it is especially critical. Our work is a lonely task. There is no one around to prod us to get it done. We are our own bosses and, if we are not good managers, the job won't get done. In other words, if you want to write, then you must write. Writing isn't accomplished in any other way. The pages will remain blank from now until infinity unless you fill them with your essence.

Edna Ferber once complained that people often came to her saying that they wanted to be writers. "Rarely," she said, "did they come to me and say, 'I want to write.' There is a great difference."

The easiest way to discipline yourself is to have a small room or space in your home where you can be alone at a set time every day and write. The purpose of setting this routine is to establish a mental habit. The mind is a computer and, as such, must be programmed to carry out your instructions to it. You must train the mind to establish good working habits. Order is important. Keep your work space neat and be neat in your work, even if neatness seems to slow you down a little in the beginning. Physical neatness is a reflection of an orderly mind.

Rule 3. Economy

Economy seems a strange word for this discussion and yet it is economical to train our minds to think purposefully and clearly. It is economical to sit down to work without procrastinating. We are all prone to making excuses for ourselves and reasons why we can't accomplish what we wish to do. In truth, excuses are excuses and there are very few, if any, valid ones. An excuse is a state of procrastination. The rule of economy states that in order to succeed, we must not indulge in procrastination. We must *Align Our Actions With Our Dreams*.

The rule of economy also states that success is the result of establishing goals for ourselves. Ask yourself:

★ What do I wish to achieve?

★ How soon do I wish to achieve it?

Goals are only target points for us. If necessary, we can change them.

One of the most important aspects of the rule of economy is the standard it sets for us. Economy doesn't allow our past mistakes or our fear of failure to stand in the way. It permits us to find the shortest distance between the two points-our efforts and our goals-and to take action.

Rule 4. Silence

Pulitzer Prize-winning novelist Shirley Ann Grau gave this answer

19

to an interviewer who questioned her about her next book. "I've started another novel," Grau admitted but refused to say another word about it, explaining that she was rather superstitious. "If you talk about a thing, you tend to lose the tension that is absolutely necessary to pull it out of you. If you talk about a book, you don't write. If you talk, you don't do."

In comparison, I know a man who has a fantastic plot for a mystery novel. He first got the idea many years ago and it has always been his intention to write the story. But instead, in his excitement, he tells the story to nearly everyone he meets. We have discussed the necessity of silence on a number of occasions but he still thinks keeping quiet about a good idea is nonsense. Six years have passed and he's still talking about it. He hasn't written a word of the story.

The evening news told the story of how the police department in a large metropolitan area mailed letters promising Super Bowl tickets to all the wanted criminals in their city. The tickets were to be given out on a specific day. When the day to pick up the tickets arrived, all those with the special letters were gathered in a designated room. Finally, when everyone was present, the police burst into the room with machine guns and rounded up the criminals. It was a great scheme to apprehend the criminals and one that could have been used over and over again. There was only one thing wrong. Instead of keeping quiet, the police had so much fun bragging about their tactics that they released the story on national television. Now that everyone knows about it, including those criminals still at large, you can bet the same idea will not be as effective again.

Another reason for maintaining silence about our work is that, being human, we all have opinions about everything. The person you tell your idea to is no exception. It is a law of physics that for every action there is an equal and opposite reaction. If you are positive about an idea, the person you tell will most often express a negative reaction. He or she may say something positive but, in thought at least, there will be an opposite reaction. This doesn't happen because the other person intends to offend you in any way, but rather because the human mind obeys the law of physics just like everything else on earth.

Whether we believe it or not, *Thoughts Are Things*. It is thinking that spurs the consciousness to action. Therefore, we should exercise caution in stimulating the response of others to something that is particularly dear to us. We must be careful not to allow outside influences, that is, others' opinions, likes, and dislikes, to affect us unknowingly. They can shoot down a project before it gets off the ground. Although silence is only one of the four mechanical rules, without it, there is little hope for a successful writing career. Remember this: *Silence Prods an Idea to Life*. *In Fiction, it Prods the Story Along*. Silence is truly a magical ingredient.

A Part of the Great Secret

A part of the great secret is a faculty inherent in each of us. For some, this faculty has been subdued for years. In others, it is highly developed. This faculty is *Imagination*.

When we were children most of us were teased about our vivid imaginations. We were told we were cute, daydreamers, filled with fanciful ideas, and, worst of all, we were whispered and snickered about behind our backs. We heard our elders say that we would "outgrow it" so often that we did, some of us quicker than others. I used to see wonderful things as a child. I had friends who were invisible to everyone except me and, best of all, I could play for hours on end and it didn't cost a cent.

Science is finally beginning to view imagination in its true light. *Imagination is Real*. As individuals, whatever we see actually exists for us. It is our inner sight, our spiritual viewpoint, the way we see the world around us and the dreams within us.

What We Write About Mirrors Ourselves

It is said that people in general are more aware now than they ever

21

have been. In a sense, this is true. Intellectually we are more advanced and more open to advancement. We are able to talk to one another from one point on the globe to another via the telephone. We can fly from one city to another. We can even fly to the moon. We have developed the power to destroy our entire planet in a matter of a few moments. Television has opened the door to mass communication, to news not only about our own society but the societies of the world. The stories told in the news format are not really much different from those told in television's dramatic programming. Have you ever thought about the similarities? The news reports a murder and a bit later in the evening, actors in an hour-long program dramatize a similar incident. Television programming does what it is supposed to do-reflect the interests of the mass consciousness. It depicts the level of society's consciousness in general. It's no secret that our most popular programs are crime-related or problem-riddled soap dramas. This type of entertainment agrees with the level of today's consciousness.

A truly creative writer does not write for an audience. We write to please ourselves, to allow the creative energy that would otherwise be dammed up within us to flow. What writers write is but a mirror image of themselves. The fact is we cannot write or truly communicate something that we do not understand. Understanding comes from experience, whether it be imaginary or physical. Writers are what they write. They are every character in their story-the good guy and the bad guy-and they also identify with the stories themselves. In other words, writers who write horror stories live at that level of consciousness. Mystery writers are filled with the mysteries they write. If one's writing is focused on adventure, then it is adventure that fills one's inner life. Do you get the idea?

Writing is a slow painstaking job. A scene in a movie or a book may take only a moment or two to watch or read but it may take as long as a week or more to write that scene.

Writing is living your work in slow motion. Writers may spend as much as two to ten hours a day at their craft and, even when not actually writing, they still flash on what is happening in their stories. So you can now see how very filled with mystery a mystery writer is,

how filled with horror the horror story writer is, how adventure-
some the adventure story writer is.

Personally, I couldn't write a horror story, or a mystery story either for that matter. Crime and gore don't interest me. What interests me are stories that depict human beings daring enough to meet the challenges of life with an eye toward conscious evolution. When one of my characters lights up with a new awareness, as the writer and inventor of that character, I do too.

Like other writers, I talk inwardly to my characters. I know them intimately because, as I write, I assume their roles. I am not the only writer who works this way. Assuming the roles of one's characters is the way most writers write; it's the ingredient that breathes life into the characters and the story. You can bet that if I have to live the lives of my characters, I am going to develop characters who appeal to me, those who, in the long run, will teach me something that I want to know. It's like choosing one's friends. We choose them because of an affinity we feel for them, a common ground where we can meet and enhance each other's lives. Likewise, I like to write uplifting stories. That way, even though my characters will drag me through some tough times, I know I'll come out on top in the end. I know I'll become a richer person, a more aware person, as a result of my story.

The Great Secret of Writing

The secret is simple. *Know What You Want To Achieve. Anchor Your Attention to a Vision of that Achievement* and, as you plod along, writing daily, keep your anchor there. If you are truly anchored to your dream as you work, you can't miss. It's like planting a seed in fertile soil. When finally you are finished, you know what you have. Plant an orange seed, get an orange tree. Structure yourself with an inspiring theme and the book you write will not only inspire you but it will inspire your readers.

The exercise that follows will help you tune in to yourself. Try it for a week before going on to the next chapter.

E X E R C I S E 1

Awareness Technique

Use a separate pad of paper or the workspace provided at the end of this exercise. Go into a quiet room or outdoors where no one will disturb you for at least 30 minutes. Sit quietly and look around.

What Do You See?

Note the objects, their colors (light or dark), textures, and sizes. Is there movement? Note the true shapes of things.

What Do You Hear?

Listen carefully. If you are indoors, pay special attention to the creaking or settling sounds of the house. Is there a breeze hissing in from a window somewhere? Be sure to leave the radio or tape deck off so that you can hear what is already there. If you are outdoors, listen for the sounds of birds, crickets or the rustling of bushes.

What Do You Smell?

Take a deep breath. Is the air stale or fresh? If it is stale, what does the staleness smell like? Lift the things around you and smell them. Smell the pad of paper on which you will write. Is there a scent of someone else who lives in your household in the room in which you are sitting? If you are outdoors, what does nature smell like today? Put your nose to the ground and smell the earth. Smell a blade of grass.

What Do You Feel?

Touch Things.

Use your senses (all of them) to examine your immediate environment. The trick is to keep your senses in the moment.

What are you seeing right now?

What are you hearing right now?

What are you smelling right now?

What are you touching right now?

What are you feeling right now?

Keep your senses in the moment! If your mind begins to wander and you begin to think of someone or something, past or future, that is outside of your immediate environment, shake your head vigorously to snap yourself back into the present moment. The first, second, or third time you try this exercise, you may have to shake your head 20 or 30 times but after awhile you'll get the hang of it. The important thing is not to give in to thoughts of other people or other places from the past or of meetings and places you plan to be. Keep your senses about you *now*.

Note: The pad of paper you have with you is for you to make notes on. Write individual words, not sentences or paragraphs, about what you experience. Write down what you see, what you hear, and so on. Try this exercise in the *same place* for seven days. See *Evaluation* on page 32.

Day One

1. What do you see? _____

_____

_____

_____

2. What do you hear? _____

_____

_____

_____

3. What do you smell? _____

_____

_____

_____

4. What are you touching? _____

_____

_____

_____

5. What do you feel? _____

_____

_____

_____

Day Two

1. What do you see? _____

_____

_____

_____

2. What do you hear? _____

_____

_____

_____

3. What do you smell? _____

_____

_____

_____

4. What are you touching? _____

_____

_____

_____

5. What do you feel? _____

_____

_____

_____

Day Three

1. What do you see? _____
_____
_____

2. What do you hear? _____
_____
_____

3. What do you smell? _____
_____
_____

4. What are you touching? _____
_____
_____

5. What do you feel? _____
_____
_____

Day Four

1. What do you see? _____
_____

_____

2. What do you hear? _____

_____

_____

3. What do you smell? _____

_____

_____

4. What are you touching? _____

_____

_____

5. What do you feel? _____

_____

_____

Day Five

1. What do you see? _____

_____

_____

2. What do you hear? _____

_____

_____

3. What do you smell? _____

_____

_____

4. What are you touching? _____

_____

_____

5. What do you feel? _____

_____

_____

Day Six

1. What do you see? _____

_____

_____

2. What do you hear? _____

_____

_____

3. What do you smell? _____
_____
_____
_____

4. What are you touching? _____
_____
_____
_____

5. What do you feel? _____
_____
_____
_____

Day Seven

1. What do you see? _____
_____
_____
_____

2. What do you hear? _____
_____
_____
_____

3. What do you smell? _____
_____

_____

4. What are you touching? _____

_____

_____

5. What do you feel? _____

_____

_____

_____

Evaluation

Read the instructions for Exercise 1 and then close your eyes, again reviewing the instructions from memory. Two things happen when you do this: 1) You discipline your mind to pay attention; and 2) You anchor your attention on the work you want to review.

Now open your eyes and quietly peruse your exercise notes from the last seven days. When finished, using the space provided here or a separate sheet of paper, ask yourself:

1. What did I see that was different?

2. What did I hear that was different?

3. What did I smell that was different?

4. What did I touch that was different?

5. What did I feel that was different?

6. Am I more observant now than I was seven days ago?

7. Do I feel differently about the environment I have been observing than I did seven days ago? In what way?

8. Am I more observant of the environment-at-large? In what way?

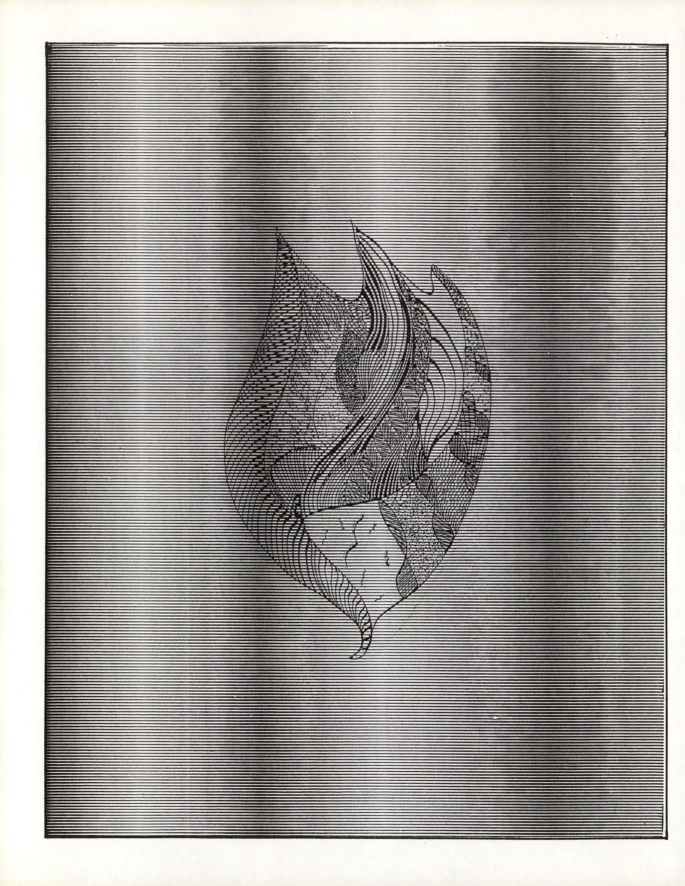

CHAPTER 2

Probing The Imagination

A dream may be defined as a succession of images passing through the mind. That being the case, a dream is with us nearly all the time. We experience dreams in one of three ways:

1. Sleep
2. Daydreams
3. Waking

The sleep dream comes to us when we close our eyes and drift into sleep. This type of dream is generally symbolic of some experience we have encountered in daily life, although the sleeping dream can also reveal the past and foretell the future, as well as introduce us to a profound mystical experience. The following story is an actual dream experience.

I was walking down an isolated road through a forest with a friend when suddenly, from out of nowhere, a brown van pulled up alongside us. The side door slid open. Two men jumped out and forced my companion and me inside.

The men, there were three of them including the driver, drove us into the city and stopped the van in front of an old brownstone house. There they told us to get out and pushed us up the concrete steps. One man unlocked the door and hurried us inside and up another flight of stairs to the second storey. They took us to the kitchen and left us, shutting the door behind them.

"We've got to get out of here," I said to my companion.

She shook her head as though she were frightened.

"Come on," I said again.

"You go on," she said nervously.

I hesitated only a moment, afraid that the men would return and it would be too late. If I got out now, I could get help. I rushed for the door, opened it, and tore downstairs and out the front door.

Directly across the street was a gas station. A security guard was calmly standing there. I ran over to him, blurting out that I had been kidnapped and that my companion was still being held prisoner in the brownstone across the street.

"Sorry, Miss," the security guard said apologetically. "I can't help you. You'll have to call the police." He pointed to a phone booth at the side of the gas station.

"But I have no money," I said.

He gave me a dime.

Panicked, I hurried to the phone and dialed the operator and told her to get me the police. She said she couldn't call them for me, that I would have to dial them for myself, and told me the number to call. But, when I hung up the phone, I was so frightened that I forgot the number she gave me and I had to get her again. This time she connected me.

In a flash, the police were there and I rushed with them back across the street, into the brownstone, and up the stairs to the second story. I stood back as they burst through the kitchen door. There was my friend, sitting with our three abductors at the kitchen table drinking coffee and laughing. I couldn't. believe my eyes.

"What's happening?" I asked. The police were standing by with their guns drawn, just as unnerved as I was.

"Oh, Heather, you take everything so seriously," my friend said.

"What do you mean?" I asked, confused.

"It was all a play, a game we made up," my friend said.

I stared at her in disbelief. It hadn't been a game to me. I had believed myself to be kidnapped and in grave danger. I had called the police to save my friend. "You can't be serious," I said finally.

She grinned and nodded her head. "It was all a game," she said again.

"Well, if it was a game, I don't want anything more to do with you," I said. "You and I are no longer friends."

She laughed and watched me leave with the police trailing behind me.

But it wasn't the last time I saw the woman. She was everywhere I went. I tried to ignore her but she always approached me with a smile, as though we were still friends. Once I turned on her. "Get out of my life," I yelled. "You and I are no longer friends. I want nothing to do with you."

"But we have to be friends," she said.

"No, we don't, and we're not," I corrected.

"But we do," she said.

"And why is that?" I asked.

"Because I am your mind!" she answered.

The next thing I knew I was sitting straight up in bed. Then it came to me: Whatever is allowed to live in the mind will come to pass; that is, the images passing through the mind, combined with feelings, produce our experiences in the environment. My dream had explained it all to me.

Daydreams

Daydreams are waking fantasies. We can produce them by sitting calmly and staring into space or while doing a physical activity, such as walking or driving. Surely you have had the experience of driving along the highway, totally forgetful of where you are, thinking about something that has happened, is happening, or could happen.

What produces a daydream? A succession of images passing through the mind. Creative writing is nothing more than a daydream written down. When we are writing a story, an article, or even an office memo, we must first view the images that show us what we want to say before we can write effectively. This is not the only way to write but, when we can first see them in our minds' eyes, the written words will be much clearer to the reader. If a writer's finished work is not clear, it is because it was unclear to the writer when it was being written.

Creative Writing Is a Daydream Written Down

Now we can understand why it is that one writer will write romance stories, while another will write horror, another adventure, and still another mysteries. We write according to the nature of the images passing through our minds.

It is important to note that once we become aware of the images passing through our minds, and we must become aware of them if we are to be capable writers, we can change them. Since we are the creators, we can erase them and replace them with images that are more to our liking. Remember, we create in the environment according to the nature of the images passing through our minds. If the images tell us we are in financial difficulty or troubled in some other way, we will project these images into the life we are living and into the words we are writing. If, on the other hand, our images are uplifting, our lives and our writings will be uplifting. A person who writes horror stories is filled with fear and horror. A person who writes romance stories is a romantic. A person who writes adventure stories is an adventurer. Of course, we're speaking in generalities. There are many types of horror stories, romance and adventure stories and there are many factors involved in each individual creation.

As a child, whenever I felt unhappy or pressured, I would reflect on a painting that used to hang in our living room. It was a woodland scene with a cozy cottage tucked in among the trees. Alongside it

38

was a fast-flowing stream. As I imagined the place, my fears would melt away and my spirits would lift. Then I would forget about my secret place until the next time I needed to go there.

Oddly enough, after I married, my husband and I moved into a house in the forest. Oak Creek passed through the property. The place was almost identical to my childhood daydream hideout. It was then that I began to realize that daydreams do become reality.

Imagination

An individual's imagination is the force that produces the succession of images passing through his or her mind. Not long ago I met a woman who told me how, when walking through a ponderesa forest she became fascinated with the long pine needles that had fallen there. She reached down to the ground, gathered a few in her hands and began to toy with them with her fingers. Bending them this way and that, she saw that they could be used to weave a tiny basket. Her first attempt was crude but there were many after that and today the woman is a professional pine needle basket maker. Her objects of art sell for four and five hundred dollars apiece.

Think back to the exercise at the end of Chapter 1. Did the imaginative faculty influence you as you worked the exercise? That is, were you experiencing a succession of images passing through your mind? What did those images report to you? Reread your notes from the exercise before you continue with this chapter.

The difference between you and me, between each of us, is our imaginative faculties. We see through our imaginations according to our individual experiences. Consequently, one individual will create baskets out of pine needles, while another will use yarn or straw. Imagination, or the succession of images passing through our minds, is the faculty of creation. Many of us have difficulty expressing our creativity because, when we were children, the strength of our imaginations was belittled by such adult phrases as, "she has such a

39

vivid imagination" when we would try to explain an experience that went deeper than what everyone else could see and touch. In truth, where would the world be without imagination, the succession of images that passed through the minds of Thomas Edison or the Wright Brothers, to name a few?

Here's an interesting thought. If imagination is real and fiction is a manifestation of imagination, then what is fiction? Fiction is nothing more than reality disguised. Fiction is a tale of the writer's experience, dressed in another costume, using other names, places, and events. All the writer's feelings and discoveries and awarenesses are embedded in the fiction. They have to be or else what they are writing about will have no life of its own. Writers fuse themselves into their work. It is this fusion that conveys interest and feeling to the reader. Without it, the work would be boring and lifeless.

What Do We Mean When We Say That Writing Can Be A Tool For Self-Discovery?

To writers who write from the depths of themselves, the statement is self-evident. You feel what you write. You experience what you write and you discover yourself through it.

One of the easiest and most profound ways to use writing as a tool for self-discovery is to keep a daily journal. At the same time every day, make note of the events that have occurred and what they meant to you. Honesty is the key here-to be true to ourselves, admitting what really occurred and what it really meant to us.

In the *Wizard of Oz*, Dorothy uses her dream experiences to work through the horrible problems of her outer life. The friendly farm hands become helpful companions on the other side, just as they are in real life. The wicked witch is the horrible old spinster who tries to take her dog Toto from her.

There are many such books that have been written as a tool for

40

self-discovery and, interestingly enough, they are books that endure through time; that is, they are always timely, passed on from generation to generation. Why? Because they contain an individual's truth and that truth, although individual, speaks to the universal mind within us all. At the end of this chapter you will find a partial reading list to help illustrate this point. Most of the books are available at your public library.

Is Imagination A Creative Tool?

Yes, but it is more than a mere tool. It is the essence of creativity.

Does A Tool Contain Power?

If I give you a hundred dollars, am I giving you power? The coin or paper of the money has no value unless you give it value, unless you use it.

What Designates The Power Of A Tool?

The tool must be used. Use of the tool taps its power. If you write frequently, you will become a better writer than someone who writes occasionally. There are several reasons for this: 1) The more you write, the more comfortable you will become with words; 2) The more you write, the freer the imagination will become. Consider the garden hose that has been left disconnected, lying on the ground through a rainy winter. When it is first connected and the

41

water is turned on, most likely the water will be muddy before it runs clear. The same is true for someone whose skills have not been exercised for some time.

A friend of mine is a cellist. Very often he is required to go out of town for a week or two at a time. When he returns, he claims it takes extraordinary effort to regain control of the instrument. His fingering is stiff and the cello feels uncomfortable next to his body. He has to go through a warm-up period to feel at home with it again. Good working habits are imperative for the writer. The more we write the more refined our work will become.

The purpose of a tool is to open and free the imagination. How then do we use writing as a tool for self-discovery?

Like Dorothy in the land of Oz, we create a situation on paper that parallels a situation in life. When we find ourselves stuck in a situation, we write an article about it, or we allow the characters in our story to work through it for us. As writers, we may wonder about something and let our article or story explore and discover it. In doing so, we can discover what we wanted to know.

Two Rules Govern Our Writing

Rule 1:

Show, don't tell. Use the action in a story or a word illustration to explain.

Rule 2:

Be objective. Allow your creations to live. Permit your characters to grow and awaken, to break out of set habits or patterns.

What Happens When Writers Take A Subjective View In Their Writing?

We become sympathetic, even impassioned, and lose foresight. When we do this, we have allowed our personal concepts of morality to block our visions of what we are trying to say.

A sculptor I know carves figures of American Indians. His early work showed a certain fascination and reverence toward them. But then something happened. The sculptor suffered the loss of a loved one in his life and blamed the Indians for his loss. He became bitter toward them and, as a result, he began to depict them as depraved figures. Instead of carving the lively statues he had done, he now shows them as murderers and thieves. The sculptor is on a downhill trend. The images passing through his mind are warping his art.

How Do The Senses Interact With Imagination?

Refer to Exercise 1 at the end of Chapter 1. What pictures did your senses produce in your mind's eye?

How Does An Outside Stimulus, Such As Music, Interact With Imagination?

Music is imagery set to the motion of sound. Words are pictures in letter form. Both are physical stimuli and, as such, can be considered tools. We can use them in a variety of ways. For instance, writers can read something and be inspired to write, and they can also listen to music and be inspired. Sometimes a shopping spree or a walk along the beach provides the stimulus that is needed. It is not the tool that provides the creative stimulus, but how a tool interacts with our imagination. Tools can be useful in prodding the imagination to see in a relaxed manner. They can set up mental diversions that will broaden our inner field of vision and, as a result, we concentrate better.

When I am under pressure to write, I often sit with my cassette headset, listening to New Age music as I work. It tends to lessen the tensions and helps me to focus in on my project better. At other times I need to withdraw myself completely, and so I'll head for a favorite meadow in the mountains near my home. When I return to my word processor, I am refreshed and ready to resume work. Diversions, however, should never be used as an escape from disciplining one's self to produce. They are merely tools that assist in the creative process.

What Is Memory And How Does It Relate To The Imagination?

Memory is imagination solidified. This is why there are so many repeated storylines and why history is continually repeating itself as well. There are areas in individual and mass consciousness that are frozen in time, stuck in a comfortable nitch, and the phonograph needle is playing over and over again in the same groove.

A perfect example of a stuck imagination is television. Have you ever wondered why there are so many crime stories? People get used to seeing them. It takes little effort to shift one's attention from one story to the next, and the networks likewise find it cost efficient to stick with them. No truly new scripts have to be written. No real thought is needed about the product. Change a little here and shift a little there and show the same program all over again. All the while, a few complain but no one seems able to break through the stuck imagination of the mass audience.

What Are Facsimiles And How Do They Relate To The Writer?

In *The Flute of God*, Paul Twitchell describes facsimiles as "little units of energy" gathered around the mind. He explains that these units of energy are pictures borrowed from our parents' attitudes, social customs, schools, books we have read, movies, and life situations we have witnessed. Whenever something stimulates our emotions, our imaginations become excited and form a picture, which is then filed away as an experience. But facsimiles are not actually our own experiences, they are borrowed ones.

When we get caught up in a TV soap opera, we are experiencing a facsimile. The feeling that we can't wait for the next episode tells us that our emotions are hooked and that we are relating to that experience as though it were our own.

Children parrot the behavior and feelings of their parents. If you want to know how a person feels about you, say hello to his or her child. If the child is warm and friendly, most likely that's how the parent feels about you. If the child is standoffish or unfriendly, then you know where you stand with the parents.

A woman I know was married for more than fifty years when her husband suddenly died. As the following months passed, the woman slowly began to change. She had obviously been greatly influenced by the attitudes of her husband and, now that he was gone, she was beginning to come into her own identity, which had been hidden.

As you may imagine, we, as writers can use facsimiles to benefit our work. We can do this by listening to the impressions of others about places, people, and things we can't possibly investigate first hand. With a little research, we can safely adapt these facsimiles to enrich our work. We can translate daily experiences - what we see, hear, and feel from others - into what we are writing. We come to recognize that life is a process of *Inner/Outer* motion and, when we do, we become aware of the waking up process in the human being.

Points To Contemplate

★ There is no original thought, so don't try to "think" yourself into the imaginative state.

★ When you try to analyze or define art, the meaning is transformed. Enjoy it for what it means to you.

★ Don't be afraid to take a big step. *You can't cross a chasm in two short jumps*.

★ No one can make you feel inferior without your consent.

★ If you wonder about the consciousness of a writer, read his or her work. Likewise, if you wish to know someone, ask to share their fantasies or dreams.

N O T E S

Daydreaming A Scene

Give yourself a fictional name. Listen inwardly to discover what it should be but try not to use the name of anyone you know personally. Preferably, use the name of someone you don't know at all.

Close Your Eyes.

With your eyes closed, *Listen* and *Watch*. At first the image will be faint but then you will see your fictional character, who is you in another form, standing before you. Although you may have heard nothing at first, now that you are seeing your fictional character you will also hear the sounds in your character's environment.

What do you hear?

What do you see?

What does he or she look like?

Is the individual alone?

What is he/she doing?

What is the setting?

Why is your fictional character there? Does he or she want to do something? Let him or her do it.

What is happening?

Open your eyes and write what you saw in one short, crisp paragraph.

_____

_____

_____

_____

_____

_____

_____

E X E R C I S E 3

Photograph Technique

Clip three photographs from a magazine or book. Make sure they
are photographs that are striking to you. Put the first one in front of
you and contemplate it, daydreaming yourself into the picture.
Who are you? What are you doing? What do you see, hear, feel,
smell, and touch? Write a short paragraph, no more than 10 lines
(preferably typed) about it. Follow this procedure with each
photograph.
   1. *Be objective.*
   2. *Be simple and direct.*
   3. *Be as plain-spoken as possible.*

_____

_____

_____

_____

_____

_____

_____

_____

_____

_____

_____

_____

_____

_____

2150 A.D.	Thea Alexander
MEDICINE WOMAN FLIGHT OF THE SEVENTH MOON.	Lynn V. Andrews
JONATHAN LIVINGSTON SEAGULL ILLUSIONS	Richard Bach
THE GIRL OF THE SEA OF CORTEZ	Peter Benchley
THE KIN OF ATA ARE WAITING FOR YOU	Dorothy Bryant
THE SACRED STONES (TRILOGY): THE TALL STONES TEMPLE OF THE SUN SHADOW ON THE STONES	Moyra Caldecott
TEACHINGS OF DON JUAN	Carolos Castaneda
THE DREAMSTONE	Cherryh
ARDATH ROMANCE OF TWO WORLDS	Marie Corelli
THE LAST BARRIER	Reshad Feild
THE QUEST FOR THE FARADAWN	Richard Ford
BLUEBIRDS	David W. Frasure
INITIATION	Elizabeth Haich
THE GLASS BEAD GAME STEPPENWOLF DEMIAN BENEATH THE WHEEL THE JOURNEY TO THE EAST SIDDHARTHA NARCISSUS & GOLDMUND ROSSHALDE	Hermann Hesse
THE GOLDEN DREAM THE SEDONA TRILOGY: THROUGH THE CRYSTAL DOORWAYS BETWEEN THE WORLDS LAND OF NOME	Heather Hughes-Calero

51

Writing As A Tool for Self-Discovery	THE BOOK OF ECK PARABLES SOUL TRAVELERS OF THE FAR COUNTRY	Harold Klemp
	A WRINKLE IN TIME A WIND IN THE DOOR A SWIFTLY TILTING PLANET	Madeleine L'Engle
	PRINCESS & THE GOBLIN PRINCESS & CURDIE	George MacDonald
	PRINCE OMBRA	Roderick MacLeish
	THE SECRET	Adrian Malone
	THE RAZOR'S EDGE	W. Somerset Maugham
	THE WAY OF THE PEACEFUL WARRIOR	Dan Millman
	TO A GOD UNKNOWN	John Steinbeck
	THE FLUTE OF GOD EAST OF DANGER TALONS OF TIME THE TIGER'S FANG THE WAY OF DHARMA STRANGER BY THE RIVER	Paul Twitchell
	MIPAN	Yongden

CHAPTER 3

Breaking The Writer's Block/ Working With Patterns

Getting Started

Take a minute and close your eyes. Contemplate why you find it difficult to get started on a writing project.

What are your reasons?

What do you feel as you pull out a blank sheet of paper and put it in your typewriter or when you turn on your computer to begin writing?

It may be that you have to develop the discipline of concentration, to be able to focus on what it is you want to do. A good method for developing concentration is to sit quietly in a comfortable position and visualize what it is you want to achieve. See what you plan to write in your mind's eye. Most likely what you write later will be different from what you contemplate, but no matter. The idea is simply to enjoy daydreaming your work to life. About fifteen or twenty minutes is enough.

What Is Writer's Block?

Our greatest enemy is tension. In Book One of *The Sedona Trilogy*, a young man named Rian relates that "Illusion comes in the form of stress, born from it and exists with it." He goes on to say that, "Sarpent, the Elder of the Great One always reminded me to relax, to avoid the tensions and expectations of others." I have learned that the less I strain my mind, the more it contacts the higher power that works for me and through me.

Tension is a fear of failure or a fear of success, or even both. Most of us fear that someone we care about will not approve of what we write and this fear cuts off the flow of creativity. Simply, writer's block is a deviation from being yourself.

There are ways to avoid tension. First, we must recognize it, know where it comes from and then dismiss it. We must establish good working habits so that we gain confidence in ourselves. In other words, we must write daily. Soft, soothing background music is also a useful tool for relaxation.

Tools Of The Artist

When we speak of the arts, we speak of all the arts, including writing, painting, sculpting, and music. In a way, they are all the same but in our society we tend to separate them.

Let's consider how those from other areas of the arts overcome their creative blocks. If you go into an art museum, you'll see people with sketch pads, noting the shadows, forms, and textures of great works of art. The painter and the sculptor know that the easiest way to learn is to study those who have already learned. This studying is done by copying, not line for line, but the essence of rhythm and motion contained in the work of art. Once the rhythm and motion of a work of art is deciphered, the artist no longer copies it. The artist has become integrated with the technique. So a painter studies the styles of other painters. A sculptor studies other sculptors' work. Oftentimes photographs will be used for these studies. Today many artists are also fine photographers. Not only do they photograph another's work but they photograph nature and then paint from that photograph.

Another popular method used by artists is the projection of an image by means of an opaque projector onto a canvas. They then paint from that projection. Although the basic form is copied, it is interesting to note that the finished product may look nothing like the piece that was projected onto the canvas. The projected piece was merely a tool to alleviate the artist's tension. Once the work of art was under way, it became an original work of art.

Musicians work the same way. They study other musicians' music until they arrive at an understanding of how it was created, that is, they can feel the essence of the movement in the notes. From there the study merely serves as a springboard for their own creations.

Each artist seeks out the patterns of other artists and uses that discovery to stimulate their own work, understanding that the true definition of originality is individual expression.

Can you remember someone who greatly influenced your life?

What effect did that person have on you?

Do you still carry that effect with you today?

What would be another name for that effect? (*Facsimile*.)

Formula Writing

Formula writing is writing that never deviates from a set pattern. It is like a mold that sculptors use to reproduce their work. Newspapers use the *Who, What, When, Where, Why* formula for news articles. Even most feature writing has a particular construction although it has a freer style. The romance novel unfolds from a set pattern just as the gothic novel does. Many mysteries also follow a set story pattern. That's why you can pick up a book, read a few chapters, and know what's going to happen next and how it is going to end. Even the most original writers have a style and a pattern to their work and, although it may be more difficult to guess where their work will lead us next, the writer's method still exists.

Life is a living series of patterns. All of life participates. Rocks and plants live relative to their environments. They take on the characteristics of those environments. For example, a species of plant living in California will look different from the same species living in Hawaii. An animal takes on the characteristics of its master. Children consciously play the roles of adults, in particular their parents. Facsimiles develop. Tiny units of energy transfer from one mind to another. There is no judgment here, only the observation that without facsimiles, without patterns, physical life could not exist.

Why is it then that writers never speak openly about studying another writer's work, about using patterns such as the painter, the sculptor, and the musician use? Writers seem to attach a stigma to this practice, afraid that they will hear the cry of plagiarism. Remember, everything already exists. Original work is an individual interpretation of what already exists.

Before we begin working with patterns, I have a few important questions to ask you. Think about the questions before reading the comments I have provided. Stay with it until you have thought them through.

It Is Said That A Good Writer Is An Honest Writer. What Does That Statement Mean?

Be true to yourself. Say what you mean and feel. Don't beat around the bush. Be direct.

Do You Have Difficulty Editing Your Own Work? For What Reason? Are You Subject To Word Fixations?

Attachment to a choice of words can destroy a piece of writing. When I was learning to write, a literary agent took an interest in me. Every week I would bring chapters of my book to Ralph Schmidt and every week he would mutilate it with his red pencil. Finally, after a year and a half, I had "gotten it right." I hated the man and loved him at the same time. Although the book that he worked on with me was never published, his often brutal red slashes over my words and paragraphs formed the foundation for my work today.

How Does A Writer Breath Life Into His or Her Characters?

If you are tense, use your tension to prod the story along. Allow your characters to feel tense. By doing so you will work through the difficulty, both for yourself and your characters. They breathe your air. Don't forget that!

When I was writing *Land of Nome*, I reached a point when I did not want to continue writing the story. Instead of quitting, I used the feeling. In the story the character Deetra hesitated at the foot of the mountain, found the next step difficult, and wished that she did not have to take it.

Patterns and How To Use Them

Now we begin working with patterns. Like the painter, sculptor, and musician, we are going to zero in on sections of other artists' work for the purpose of understanding their rhythms and forms. You will notice that I have chosen writers with different styles. The material used is from the first few paragraphs of each writer's book. In the section called PATTERN 1, I have given you an example of how an adaptation might be done. The idea is to substitute your own story and your own words in place of those already written.

EXERCISE 4

Using Patterns

Pattern 1

"The naked child ran out of the hide-covered lean-to toward the rock beach at the bend in the small river. It didn't occur to her to look back. Nothing in her experience ever gave her reason to doubt the shelter and those within it would be there when she returned.

She splashed into the river and felt rocks and sand shift under her feet as the shore fell off sharply. She dived into the cold water and came up sputtering, then reached out with sure strokes for the steep opposite bank. She had learned to swim before she learned to walk and, at five, was at ease in the water. Swimming was often the only way a river could be crossed."

from *Clan of the Cave Bear* by Jean Auel
(Copyright © 1980 by Jean M. Auel. Used by permission of
Crown Publishers, Inc.)

Adaptation of Pattern 1

"The dark-skinned man stepped out of the hollow of the giant redwood tree and hurried toward the meadow at the bend in the narrow trail. It didn't occur to him to look back. Nothing in his experience ever gave him reason to doubt the tree and the forest around it would be there when he returned.

He called into the meadow and heard his echo come back from the sharp cliffs beyond. He let out a shrill whistle and called again and was met with an echo and another voice, then shouted in a clear voice that he was coming. He had learned to always announce himself to the meadow folk and, once that was done, knew he was welcome. The meadow was the only place he knew to go outside the forest."

Pattern 2

"At daybreak Billy Buck emerged from the bunkhouse and stood for a moment on the porch looking up at the sky. He was a broad, bandy-legged little man with a walrus mustache, with square hands, puffed and muscled on the palms. His eyes were a contemplative, watery gray and the hair which protruded from under his Stetson hat was spiky and weathered. Billy was still stuffing his shirt into his blue jeans as he stood on the porch. He unbuckled his belt and tightened it again. The belt showed, by the worn shiny places opposite each hole, the gradual increase of Billy's middle over a period of years. When he had seen to the weather, Billy cleared each nostril by holding its mate closed with his forefinger and blowing fiercely. Then he walked down to the barn, rubbing his hands together. He curried and brushed two saddle horses in the stalls, talking quietly to them all the time; and he had hardly finished when the iron triangle started ringing at the ranch house. Billy stuck the brush and currycomb together and laid them on the rail, and went up to breakfast. His action had been so deliberate and yet so wasteless of time that he came to the house while Mrs. Tiflin was still ringing the triangle. She nodded her gray head to him and withdrew into the kitchen. Billy Buck sat down on the steps, because he was a cow-hand, and it wouldn't be fitting that he should go first into the dining-room. He heard Mr. Tiflin in the house, stamping his feet into his boots."

The Red Pony by John Steinbeck

Adaptation of Pattern 2

(You write.)

_____

_____

_____

Pattern 3

The girl lay on the surface of the sea, looking into the water through a mask, and was afraid.

    She was surprised to feel fear-a true, deep fear that bordered on panic-for not in years had anything in the sea frightened her.

But then, never in her life had she been actively, aggressively menaced by an animal. Creatures had snapped at her, and some had circled her, hungry and curious, but always a show of strength and confidence had sent them on their way in search of more appropriate prey.

But this animal did not seem to want to bite her, or eat her. It looked to her as if it wanted simply to hurt her, to stab her.

It appeared with magical speed. One moment the girl was gazing into an empty blue haze; the next, she was staring at a sharp and pointed bill of bone that quivered three feet from her chest. The bill swooped back to a broadened base, and ended in two clam-size black eyes as cold as night."

The Girl of The Sea of Cortez by Peter Benchley

Adaptation of Pattern 3

(You write.)

_____

_____

_____

_____

_____

_____

_____

_____

_____

_____

_____

_____

_____

_____

_____

_____

_____

_____

_____

_____

_____

_____

Pattern 4

"There are dragons in the twins' vegetable garden."

Meg Murry took her head out of the refrigerator where she had been foraging for an after-school snack, and looked at her six-year-old brother. "What?"

"There are dragons in the twins' vegetable garden. Or there were. They've moved to the north pasture now."

Meg, not replying-it did not do to answer Charles Wallace too quickly when he said something odd-returned to the refrigerator. "I suppose I'll have lettuce and tomato as usual. I was looking for something new and different and exciting."

"Meg, did you hear me?"

A Wind in the Door by Madeleine L'Engle

Adaptation of Pattern 4

(You write.)

_____

_____

_____

_____

_____

_____

_____

_____

_____

_____

_____

_____

_____

_____

_____

_____

_____

_____

_____

_____

_____

Pattern 5

He stood before his mahogany shaving stand, stirred his brush in the white shaving bowl with blue flowers which sat on a circular shelf, added hot water from a copper jug, lathered his light-complected face and then opened his finely honed steel razor with its ebony handle.

For twenty-two-year-old Charles Darwin shaving was a pleasant, hardly arduous task since he wore his reddish-brown sideburns full to the angle of his jawbone. All he had to clear was his ruddy cheeks and fully rounded chin. His red lips were a bit small compared to the remarkable stretch of his brown and purple-specked eyes which observed and recorded everything.

The Origin by Irving Stone

Adaptation of Pattern 5

(You write.)

_____

_____

_____

_____

_____

_____

_____

_____

_____

_____

_____

_____

_____

_____

_____

_____

_____

_____

_____

_____

_____

_____

Pattern 6

"It was a quiet morning, the town covered over with darkness and at ease in bed. Summer gathered in the weather, the wind had the proper touch, the breathing of the world was long and warm and slow. You had only to rise, lean from your window, and know that this indeed was the first real time of freedom and living, this was the first morning of summer.

Douglas Spaulding, twelve, freshly wakened, let summer idle him on its early-morning stream. Lying in this third-story cupola bedroom, he felt the tall power it gave him, riding high in the June wind, the grandest tower in town. At night, when the trees washed together, he flashed his gaze like a beacon from this lighthouse in all directions over swarming seas of elm and oak and maple. Now . . ."

Dandelion Wine by Ray Bradbury

Adaptation of Pattern 6

(You write.)

_____

_____

_____

_____

_____

_____

_____

_____

_____

_____

_____

_____

_____

_____

_____

_____

_____

_____

_____

_____

_____

**Writing As A
Tool for
Self-Discovery**

NOTES

NOTES

CHAPTER 4

Viewpoint/Attitude/ Attention

Because we live on the inside looking out, it is often difficult to realize our viewpoints on life. We require an environment to reflect what we think and feel. The environment is actually the landscape or setting for our waking dreams.

Dream: A succession of images passing through the mind.

1. Sleeping

2. Daydreaming

3. Waking (Experiencing)

Viewpoint

Viewpoint means a point of view. Writers actually have as many points of view as they have characters; that is, writers must develop the ability to see from the point of view of their creations. Of course, writers also determine the point of view from which their creations are presented.

There is an old saying that explains an individual's viewpoint as "the nature of the beast." Let's take the time now to examine that statement.

A. What is the nature of dogs? (Devotion)

B. Nature of cats? (Independent, curious)

C. Nature of birds? (Free)

D. Nature of cows? (Consistent)

E. Nature of sheep? (Timid, sensitive)

F. Nature of rats? (Greedy, sneaky)

G. Nature of horses? (Noble)

H. Nature of humans? (Combination of all)

The same type of exploration can be done with insects, plants, rocks, minerals, and the elements, only the lower the life form, the more subtle and less defined the individual natures become. This is because the lower forms of life are less evolved. The nature of the human, on the other hand, is the most highly evolved of all life forms. Because the human has passed through the evolutionary scale, having been all things, we have accumulated the natures of all things. Human beings are the combination of all living nature and have the consciousness to be devoted, independent, curious, free, consistent, timid, sensitive, greedy, sneaky, noble, and so on.

If you throw a stone at a dog, the dog will follow the stone. If you throw a stone at a lion, the lion will immediately go to the source of the stone. The stones signify frustration and anger. Human beings know this and are able to control their reactions. Animals react instinctively.

Nature and viewpoint mean the same thing on the mineral, plant, and animal levels. Humans have the ability to change their viewpoint and/or expand it. Human beings achieve this change or expansion of viewpoint through their attitudes.

Attitude

An attitude is a way of acting, feeling, or thinking. Attitudes begin to form in us when we are babies and our personalities begin to develop. This development takes place as babies begin to be aware of other people and the environments about them. An attitude is a tool and the tool can be used for positive or negative results.

In *The Golden Dream*, Milarepa asks his guru Marpa, "How do I take control of my mind?"

"By examining your attitudes," Marpa says. "Your attitudes are your viewpoints of life. They are the anchorpoints of your consciousness. You must first discover what they are before you can deal with them."

An attitude is formed by clinging to a feeling. The feeling then becomes an opinion and a belief. Attitudes control our view of life. When we become fixed in our attitudes, our attention becomes locked in a particular point of view. We must ask ourselves if our energy is going in the direction of our goals. To achieve what we wish to achieve, we must adjust our attitudes so that we can align our actions with our dreams. We do this by getting outside of our own houses and looking in at ourselves.

Consider This: What we see in the environment, our viewpoint (the result of our attitudes and attention), is a waking dream (a succession of images passing through the mind as we experience life).

Attitudes affect our viewpoint by limiting us. They set up barriers around our vision, like the shore of a lake. When writing, don't be rigid. Allow yourself to change and grow through your writing.

What is a rigid viewpoint to you?

A story appeared in the news about Mrs. Barfield, an elderly woman of gentle appearance, who murdered a great number of people because she felt they had no reason to live. In her final statement on the way to the gas chamber she made a public apology, not for killing the people, but for causing so much trouble to everyone in the judicial system.

Think about the attitude at work here. Mrs. Barfield was worried about what people felt toward her, rather than being concerned about what she had done.

Some members of our community got together and decided to establish a non-profit educational facility to acquaint school children with a family farm. It was an exciting idea and one that would no doubt prove valuable to the community. What slowed it down most of all, however, was the Board of Directors' insistance on making the project bigger than originally intended. Once they gave up the idea of spending millions of dollars that the organization did not have, the project began to grow. It caught public attention and support by bringing farm shows to the schools. Now it also promotes an annual sheepdog competition and is gradually gaining more and more recognition. One day they may, in fact, need a multi-million dollar facility, but the growth will come about naturally, step by step. Because the organization is now functioning from the level of its capacity, aspects of the dream are clicking into place. The dream is manifesting as the capacity expands.

Perspective is the controlling force at issue in this story. Consider how one's perspective affects one's viewpoint. There is a fine line between the two. Perspective is how you see things. Attitude is formed as a result of your perspective.

**Your writing provides you with a way of viewing things,
a way of viewing life!**

FIRST PERSON VIEWPOINT: I/ME
SECOND PERSON VIEWPOINT: YOU

THIRD PERSON VIEWPOINT: HE/SHE/THEY

Every viewpoint has an objective or subjective perspective. Overall, the tenor of both the first and second person viewpoints are subjective, but the first person may appear to be objective. If you are writing from personal experience and referring to your experience from the *I/Me* viewpoint, your writing is subjective. If you are writing from the *I/Me* viewpoint as an observer, viewing someone else's experience, then your writing is objective.

The value of writing in the first or second person is the personal, intimate quality you can project to your reader.

Hermann Hesse's *Demain* was written in the first person objective. The first-person character was the observing character (narrator), not the main character. He also wrote another book, *The Journey to the East*, in which he used the first-person subjective viewpoint. Here he tells of his quest for spiritual knowledge and how he felt as he slowly advanced along the way. It is a book that makes you feel as if you are the author, making the journey yourself.

Writing in the first person however, has its limitations. The writers see only through their own eyes. If they are the observers (objective), they watch and report what has been made obvious to them. If they are the experiencers (subjective), the limits are set by their characters' consciousness from moment to moment.

Third-person viewpoint provides a broader, less limiting outlook. It is the viewpoint of the chess player, looking down on a game in progress. The writer can study the positions of all the players, their possible moves, and what consequences they will have on each other. This viewpoint can also be subjective or objective.

Third-person subjective involves an intimacy with the main character. Its reality evolves from that character's experience. It is the technique mainly used for romance, gothic, and adventure novels, as well as many magazine, newspaper, and television features. The objective viewpoint, on the other hand, is less personal and more aloof. Most mystery writers, such as Agatha Christie, use this point of view. It presents the surface of things happening in a story and therefore keeps the reader guessing.

Viewpoint is said to be the key to all writing, fiction and non-fiction, because it presents the attitudes of the characters in fiction and the attitude by which a subject is presented in non-fiction. So you see, either way, viewpoint is the revealer, the force that lets the cat out of the bag and tells the reader what it's all about.

Earlier we spoke of the discipline required to sit down and write but there is another kind of discipline that is needed in writing. Writers have to discipline themselves to maintain a viewpoint. While a viewpoint can evolve into another viewpoint, writers have a responsibility to show it evolving. If they simply change it without justifying the change to the reader, their work will appear sloppy and out of control, a stream of consciousness that wanders aimlessly. While this type of writing has seen its day, the mass consciousness has now evolved and the modern reader would find it boring. Another point. Be strict with yourself. Edit out the unnecessary. If you have written some pretty words that have no purpose, be considerate enough of your reader to remove them.

How Does Attention Relate to Discipline?

Our attention gets pulled away from its anchorpoint when we lose our discipline. The flow of writing responds to the evolution of cycles as does the flow of life. A cycle begins. It develops with experience and then concludes. Thus, the ebb and flow gently move our attention from anchorpoint to anchorpoint and the reader can understand the continuity of what is going on between them. This type of disciplined attention from the writer allows the reader to participate in the discovery of what the writer is writing. In other words, these anchorpoints can be described as "hooks" because they arouse reader interest.

In fiction, as in life, time exists as a paradox.

Flashbacks

When confronted with a situation, the mind immediately tries to categorize it by recalling a past parallel occurrence, either from personal experience or through facsimile. The mind is a computer. When its attention is drawn to a person or thing, it immediately searches for references. If it finds none, it will project an attitude of distrust. If, on the other hand, it can find an acceptable reference, it will project an attitude of acceptance.

To the writer, these references to the past or flashbacks are invaluable. They reveal the innermost secrets of a fiction writer's characters. These innermost secrets are responsible for the characters' points of view, which are really bits and pieces of the writer's point of view. In this way, writers can see themselves and the reader sees into the characters. When a character has strong feelings about someone or something, either positive or negative, what are those feelings revealing?

Strong feelings from a character in a story, associate the character and that with which he identifies. If he strongly opposes drunkenness, it is because he has seen himself in that state, in this or another lifetime, and has disciplined himself not to drink. Similarly, the person who has smoked cigarettes for twenty years, after having quit, is disgusted by the smell of the smoke. Thus strong feelings from a character reveal aberrations the character has. We need only listen to the subtleties of what people tell us about themselves in order to know them. But now comes the most important discovery, the answer to why we are alive, living the life that we live. As long as we are attached to a particular feeling via our attitudes, we will continue to live as we have been living, until the cycle of experience is complete, or until we experience a revelation or understanding about the nature of our attitudes. The revelation experience is a joy for skillful writers. It allows them to use writing as a tool for self-discovery by allowing their subjects to discard worn-out attitudes and evolve to a higher state of consciousness.

Attitude and attention changes = Viewpoint changes

When we write, we must allow our characters to think. Thought combined with feeling produces imagery, which has an effect on the environment and on the story being told.

A. Seeing one's goals achieved produces positive effects.

B. Seeing one's failure to achieve a goal produces negative effects.

Fortune Telling

If writers truly think about what their craft has taught them, they will come to realize that the past is the present and the present is the future; that everything they write is but a reflection of themselves. With this knowledge, writers can walk into a public library, pick out any book, and *Know* the state of consciousness of the author.

E X E R C I S E 5

Patterns For Viewpoint

Use the following excerpts as patterns. Rewrite them in your own words, but maintain the viewpoint of the original author.

First Person Objective

"I noticed that Demian exerted equal fascination over the other students. I hadn't told anyone about his version of the story of Cain, but the others seemed to be interested in him, too. At any rate, many rumors were in circulation about the "new boy." If I could only remember them all now, each one would throw some light on him and could be interpreted."

Demian by Hermann Hesse

Viewpoint Pattern: First Person Objective

(*Demian* Adaptation)

_____

_____

_____

_____

_____

_____

_____

_____

_____

_____

_____

_____

_____

_____

_____

_____

_____

_____

_____

First Person Subjective

"Mila, you're not listening to me," Zesay said, turning on her heels and pouring me a cup of the thick butter-salt tea. "We could be married and move away from here. No one would know us in Katmandu. Our life would be a clean slate. My parents would give us their blessings." She hesitated, standing over me as I sat, with my head lowered, on floor cushions next to the stove. How could I tell her that such an idea was out of the question. I knew that Zesay was afraid and so was I. We had been promised to each other from birth and yet my mother could delay fulfillment of that promise for an endless time. "We are of marrying age," she said sadly.

The Golden Dream by Heather Hughes-Calero

Viewpoint Pattern: First Person Subjective

(*The Golden Dream* Adaptation)

_____

_____

_____

_____

_____

_____

_____

_____

_____

_____

_____

_____

_____

_____

_____

_____

_____

_____

_____

_____

_____

Third Person Objective

"Sir Cedric Banner entered the common room of the Westchester Club and walked directly to his chair. He seated himself as if the chair and the area about it were personal possessions, and well he might since nothing but the bottom of a Banner had touched that chair's seat for more than a half century. As he reached for his copy of the _TIMES_ from the table at his side he seemed to be looking up and over every member of the Westchester Club."

Sherlock Holmes by Sir Arthur Conan Doyle

83

Third Person Subjective (Reconstruction from above excerpt.)

"Sir Cedric Banner settled into his chair, the one vacated only last year when his father died, and picked up his copy of the *Times* from the table at his elbow. It was a fresh copy, just as his father had received the *Times* for fifty years before him."

Can you hear the subtle change from objective to subjective writing? Subjective is more personal, from the viewpoint of the character, whereas objective is an overview.

Viewpoint Pattern: Third Person Objective

(*Sherlock Holmes* Adaptation)

_____

_____

_____

_____

_____

_____

_____

_____

_____

_____

_____

_____

_____

_____

_____
_____
_____
_____
_____
_____
_____

Third Person Subjective

"Deetra stared at the path before them. What Rian remembered was true. Yet Curtser was their friend. His struggle for power seemed to be holding him and holding the villagers. And what of the Dales who were starving as a result? She tried to listen to the feelings of her heart being pulled two ways. More than life she wished the glory of entering the City of Light, of being equal to her beloved Ian and, at the same time, she knew she could find no happiness if she did not feel she had done all in her power to rescue the people and the Dales. But what could she do?"

Through The Crystal by Heather Hughes-Calero

Viewpoint Pattern: Third Person Subjective

(*Through The Crystal* Adaptation)

_____
_____
_____
_____

85

_____

_____

_____

_____

_____

_____

_____

_____

_____

_____

_____

_____

_____

_____

_____

_____

Third Person Objective

"In a hole in the ground there lived a hobbit. Not a nasty, dirty, wet hole, filled with the ends of worms and an oozy smell, nor yet a dry, bare, sandy hole with nothing in it to sit down on or to eat: it was a hobbit-hole, and that means comfort."

The Hobbit by J.R. Tolkien

Viewpoint Pattern: Third Person Objective

(*The Hobbit* Adaptation)

_____

_____

_____

_____

_____

_____

_____

_____

_____

_____

_____

_____

_____

_____

_____

_____

_____

_____

_____

_____

_____

EXERCISE 6

Viewpoint Studies: Still Life

Arrange a banana, an orange, an apple, and a pear in a bowl. Decide which one you feel is the sweetest. For the sake of illustration, let's say that you decide that the sweetest piece of fruit is the apple.

1. Write a *First Person Subjective* fantasy narrative (not merely dialogue) from the viewpoint of the apple and how sweet it believes itself to be. What does it see? What does it feel about the other fruit and itself?

2. Write a *First Person Objective* narrative from the viewpoint of one of the other pieces of fruit in the bowl. What does it see, hear, and feel about the apple.

3. Write a *Third Person Subjective* narrative using yourself as the viewpoint character. What do you see, etc.?

4. Write a *Third Person Objective* narrative of the entire situation.

Keep the narratives short and to the point, no more than ten lines each. There is space for you to work on the following pages.

Viewpoint Studies: Still Life

1. First person subjective narrative: _____

    _____

    _____

    _____

    _____

    _____

2. First person objective narrative: _____

3. Third person subjective narrative: _____

4. Thrid person objective narrative: _____

EXERCISE 7

Viewpoint Studies: Looking Glass Technique

Sometime when you are alone and quiet, go outside of your house, walk up to a window and look in. Stay there a few moments, looking around the room, and noting the items there.

1. Recognize items you have purchased and how you felt about them when you bought them.

2. What items in the room were given to you as gifts? By whom? What are your feelings about the giver and the gift?

3. Do you have a favorite chair in the room? Why?

Now change your view of the room. Be objective. Turn your back on the window, telling yourself that you are about to peer through a stranger's window.

1. Turn around. Look in. What do you see?

2. What is your overall opinion of the room?

3. Imagine that your best friend lives there and he or she has just entered the room.

4. Describe how your friend feels in that environment. Go back inside and write about it in one or two crisp paragraphs.

Viewpoint Studies: Conversation

Engage yourself in a conversation with a family member or friend.
Particularly listen to what they have to say. Are they speaking from:
> *First person subjective?*
> *First person objective?*
> *Third person subjective?*
> *Third person objective?*

During the conversation, notice if one or both of you switch
viewpoints and when it occurs. In other words, does the change in
viewpoint come about when the topic of conversation changes or
does it come about as a result of a change in opinion.

Use this exercise often. Use it throughout the day, whenever you
have the opportunity to chat with someone. Make notes in your
journal daily, not about what people said to you, but how they said it.

_____

_____

_____

_____

_____

_____

_____

_____

_____

_____

_____

_____

_____

E X E R C I S E   9

Viewpoint Studies: Public Library Technique

Now that you understand that a book is merely a reflection of the author's consciousness, walk into a public library and look around. Go to any shelf, slip your fingers around the spine of any book, and pull it out. Hold the book carefully in your hand, thinking about the fact that you are holding a bit of someone's consciousness. Respectfully open it at random and read the first paragraph that meets your eyes.

1. What does it say?

2. What viewpoint is it written in?

3. What is it about?

4. How does it make you feel? Even a textbook, like this one, projects feeling in the reader.

Close the book and then open it again at random. Go through the same process three times. Then go to another book and do the same thing. As you make your way through the library, you will become aware that books are like individuals, individuals in the sense that they are bits of human individuals in printed form.

CHAPTER 5

The Creative Process/The Winning Writer's Consciousness

The purpose of this book is to help the writer interpret
invisible rhythms in visible ones. We each set our own
limitations in accordance with our own desires. One may
be a thin wire with weak energy and carry a weak current,
another may be a heavy wire. The energy is unlimited,
but the gauge of wire varies, according to the goals we set
for ourselves.

Humility

The dictionary defines humility as "having or showing awareness of one's defeats: not self-assertive." The humility we speak of has an entirely different meaning. It means that we detach ourselves, our personality or ego, from whatever it is we want to create. When the personal ego is suppressed, a greater force moves in and takes its place. This greater force is the primal force of creation. When it

97

creates, its creation has universal appeal. Its source is unlimited. Without it, operating from personal ego alone, the well of creativity runs dry.

Sporadic writers unknowingly are slaves to their minds. They write and write and write for a day or two or three at a time and then suddenly are burnt out. The mind, which was once filled with ideas, is emptied out and wanders aimlessly in search of a new stimulus.

When writing from the higher consciousness, the source of energy is unlimited. The only way to do this, however, is for the ego to surrender its grip on things. But first we must learn to spot the ego. It is often easier to spot the ego in others than it is to see it in ourselves.

How Can You Tell If A Person You Are Talking To Is Speaking From The Personal Ego?

Easy. The personal ego, personality, mind, whatever you want to call it, is that part of ourselves that thinks in parts. Its main joy in life is in dissecting things. It'll take an already concluding idea and chew it over and over until it exhausts itself. Once the mind is agitated or excited, it's difficult to quiet it unless you know how.

The worse part of being controlled by the personal ego is that we lose foresight because we cannot see the universality of all things. When we are speaking from the personal ego, we believe ourselves to be victims of circumstance, controlled by good and bad fortune. We lose our true vision of things. We believe our afflictions to be external rather than internal, a result of what someone has done to us, rather than what we have done to ourselves.

How Can You Tell If Someone Is Speaking From The Higher Consciousness?

Like the mind, the higher consciousness has a distinct voice. Instead

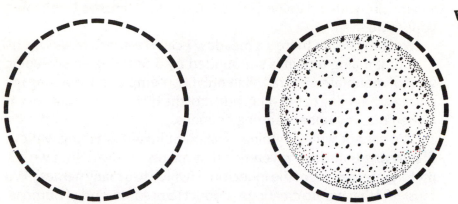

Left, seen from the whole or universal ego; Right, seeing in bits and pieces from the mind.

of seeing things in bits and pieces, however, the higher consciousness witnesses the wholeness of things. It sees everything as a whole and the words it chooses are acceptable to all personalities or egos because they are not judgmental. The higher consciousness in people speaks the truth clearly and directly. It is connected to the fountain of life and there is no end to its creativity.

Mediocrity means averageness - not very good, not very bad. To achieve greatness, one has to go beyond mediocrity. There is only an inch of difference between the two - the great and the average - but that inch is so difficult, so vast. Only the awareness of a higher power can make greatness possible. The higher power is the ego of true humility. It is the force of creation.

Reverence

Reverence is a feeling of deep respect and love. It can be achieved by looking inward to see the cause of things. To do this it is important that you be alone long enough to become truly acquainted with yourself. Learn to listen for silent messages and inner nudges. These will inspire you and guide you to interpret the images that crowd your mind.

Near my home there's a meadow I call Heather's Meadow. Its beautiful rolling terrain is surrounded by a 360 degree sweeping view of mountains. There I sit in quiet contemplation, quieting my mind and yielding to the silent music of the higher consciousness. It is then that my understanding deepens.

We cannot write anything of value or invent anything without first having that deep reverence that makes us aware that we are merely interpreters of the inner force (which has many names). We must feel that we are creating a product to fit some kind of purpose. Locked in the word "purpose" is the true meaning of reverence.

When I enter my office and begin to write, I declare myself a worthy vehicle or interpreter. Then comes the feeling, the rhythm, the meter of inspiration, and I know I am ready to work creatively. Nothing can disturb this knowledge.

Inspiration

Inspiration comes to those who seek it with humility about their achievements. When the ego claims reward for its achievements, it muses about how purposeful it is in being alive. The ego wants to make sure that everyone knows of its achievements. It is filled with self-pride. One who is truly filled with inspiration moves silently, knowing a greater power working within.

Inspiration is a gift but it is not a gift that is given without first being sought. We must first prepare ourselves to be inspired; not merely dreaming about it but aligning our actions with our dreams as well.

Love your work. Love life. Express gratitude for all that you have. Cultivate that grand, exhilarating feeling of sitting on top of a high mountain; of breathing in the high, exciting air and feeling the bubbles of joy within. Flashes of inspiration come when we are plugged into the universe and become harmonious with its rhythms.

Harmony

Vibrations around us harmonize with what we feel and project. If we feel chaos, then we project confusion. To function creatively, it is necessary that we be true to ourselves. Be true to yourself. Be true to others.

Not long after my husband and I were first married, we drove to a friend's house to attend a gathering there. My husband was uncomfortably quiet as he drove, and I looked over at him and asked, "Is something troubling you, honey?"

"No" was his reply.

We drove for another mile or two, the silence thickened, and then I prodded again. "Are you sure there's nothing wrong?"

"Well, I really don't want to go to this thing," he snapped back, hitting the steering wheel with the butt of his hand as he made his point.

"Why didn't you say so?" I asked, truly surprised. I had believed that we both agreed to visit our friends.

"Because you wanted to go," he said.

I asked my husband to turn the car around and take us home. It was not necessary for him to go anywhere he did not want to go. He had been driving in uncomfortable silence, going against the grain of his own feelings. As a result, we both suffered. Although I would have liked him to join me, it was fine with me if he didn't want to go. If I wanted to, I could go myself.

If we're not watchful, vibrations around us can affect us in a number of ways.

There are people who are energy drainers. I'm sure you've been in their presence at one time or another. As you sit down opposite

101

them and they begin to talk, your body gets heavier and heavier, sinking deeper and deeper into the chair. The skin on your face feels numb and you feel weak, almost paralyzed.

In one of his many books, Paul Twitchell cautioned that "a split mind rings like a cracked bell." I don't believe I fully understood that statement until one day, when I was returning home from the market. My two small dogs were asleep in the back seat. I was disturbed that I had given my word to attend a beach party in honor of someone I found disagreeable. I didn't want to go and, all the way home, I thought about excuses to cancel out. As I pulled into our driveway, one of the little dogs began to cry. They had been in the car a long while and I assumed that he was in a hurry to be freed in his yard. Before pulling into the garage, I opened the car door and let the little guy out, watching him run for the grass as I slowly headed for the garage. As I rolled the car onto the concrete pad in the garage, I was still absorbed in my predicament. Suddenly, I was interrupted by a flashing image of my little dog under the back wheel of the car. There was a thump and I knew that I had heard the inner warning too late. I jumped from the car. My little dog was still alive but injured.

Instantly, I understood what had happened. My mind's attention had been split between what was happening in the *Now* and what I was trying to ward off in the future. Twitchell's warning had come home.

Early in his training, the great adept Milarepa learned about the nature of accidents from his guru. In *The Golden Dream*, Milarepa complains to his guru Marpa about an accident he has had. "Accidents do not exist," Marpa told him. He then went on to say, "The word accident is an excuse invented by man to avoid facing up to the cause of an incident. In your case the cause was split attention."

A little later on in the story, Marpa explains further. "Accidents and misfortune go hand in hand for the average man who does not understand spiritual law. In truth, accidents and misfortune are mere reflections of a person's attention. The quality of one's attention is the determining factor of the outcome. A person who holds his attention on negative thoughts will draw circumstances to himself according to the intensity of his thoughts." This is exactly what I had done. In thinking negatively, inventing excuses to avoid a previous commitment, my attention was split and I hurt something that I loved very much.

Desire

All great writers have had a burning desire to write, just as all great inventors have been absorbed in their ideas. Desire, however is a double-edged blade. Without desire we can achieve nothing and yet, if we desire too strongly, we push the object of our desire from us. When an electrical plug is put into a socket, the electricity flows, but if the appliance uses 110 volts and is plugged into a 220 volt socket, it will burn up.

Intuition

Intuition is a hunch or a nudge that is spurred on by a sense of knowing. A sense of knowing is quite different from a sense of knowledge in that knowledge is something that is recognized. It comes from direct experience, books, or other facsimiles. Knowledge is ours for the asking, but we have to ask for it. A sense of knowing, on the other hand, is something that is understood without apparent reason or logic. It is a room illuminated by the light of the Soul. We know and we know we know but we can't explain how we know it. It is the force that nudges intuition. Intuition cannot voice itself in a crowded mind. To make use of it, we must be relaxed long enough to give it a chance to speak out.

Inner Silence

Without inner silence there can be no creativity. From it stems intuition, inspiration, reverence, humility, and so on. Learn to adopt a listening attitude as you move through your day. (See Exercise 11 at the end of this chapter.) We need time to ourselves, to be alone. If there is no opportunity to walk off into nature, then go into a room alone and shut the door behind you. If being alone isn't possible, as you drink a cup of coffee or sip tea, gaze into the bottom of your cup and focus your attention there. For one split second, you can isolate yourself even though there are others around you.

Is A Person Limited By His Or Her So-Called Ability?

No. Our ability can be magnified by the constant realization of our unity with the source. When we develop spiritually, everything about us is heightened, including our intelligence and the capacity to apply it.

What Is The Power Of Realization?

Realization keeps us exalted and excited with inspiration. It focuses our attention and protects us from distractions, including disease, accidents, and misfortunes. It is the awakening of the true identity or self. It is power, not the personal ego power but the creative power.

Constant realization makes life easier. We look better. Our walk acquires a lightness and we seem to be more dynamic and attractive. A special light shines in the eyes of one who lives in a state of constant realization.

Aligning Our Actions With Our Dreams

Often, we are caught up in our dreams of being writers but we do not act accordingly. We want to be writers but we don't write. The way to align our actions with our dreams is to develop inner silence, which we will discuss in the next chapter, and to establish a goal and a plan for action.

A plan is a mold that can be filled. Without a plan the energy, the divine energy, remains scattered. To create, we must direct the energy.

Thinking is a dynamic state that allows us to see patterns, forms, and images in the formless universe. Thinking sometimes causes us difficulty when it doubles back on an idea and cancels it with mental aberrations and over-analysis.

Joy

Joy is the compensating principle of balance. It renews us with creative energy after we have done creative work. Joy recharges us with enough balancing energy for the next achievement. For instance, a belittled child may grow up to have no confidence. One who is encouraged may become an achiever.

Poverty is a state of mind. By poverty, we do not mean having no money. A friend of mine grew up in a family of nine. He often tells how his family had no money but considered themselves wealthy because they had so much love for one another. Poverty is the result of inner dullness. A person in a state of poverty cannot utilize

105

the experience of joy. Joy stems from a balance of both giving and receiving. People who are in a state of poverty believe they have nothing to give and focus only on what they can get. They are on the receiving end only.

When we dislike our work, we live in a state of poverty because life becomes drudgery. Average office workers experience a lack of freedom in the nine-to-five world. Every few weeks the confined workers take a day off just to recharge their batteries. Otherwise they would go through life devitalized and drained. Many people do live in this state and, as the years go by, their minds become dull and their bodies age before their time.

We can draw energy to ourselves through joy and by being true to ourselves. The greater the joy, the greater the charge of energy we receive and the better job we do. A truly joyful person is one who is dynamic but calm, humble, and reverent and supremely happy and purposeful. Great writers, as well as great composers, painters, sculptors, inventors, politicans, engineers, doctors, and so on all face their work with inner joyfulness. Joyful people are almost always leaders in their fields. Their joyfulness is a quiet joyfulness that makes others feel comfortable in their presence.

**The purpose of this course is to help you interpret
invisible rhythms in visible ones.**

E X E R C I S E   10

Making The Invisible Visible

Go through your local newspaper and look for a photograph that has another photograph printed directly behind it on the next page. Clip it out. The one I found is a photograph of a man (but any subject will do) and, on the other side is a picture of a mountain cabin with trees in the background (again, any picture will do).

Hold the newspaper photo up to the light, preferably in front of a window so that the sun can shine through it. Notice how one image overlaps the other. In the photograph I clipped from the newspaper, it appears that the man is superimposed over the mountain cabin, as though the mountain cabin were an image he carried in his imagination. That's the point of this exercise - to become aware that what we carry in our imaginations is with us in the invisible realm.

E X E R C I S E   11

Finding The Inner Voice

Close yourself in a quiet room or go off to the woods where you can be alone. Tilt your head slightly and then close your eyes.

Listen.

What do you hear?

Picture the sounds around you. You may hear a bird chirp and see the image of the bird in your imagination. Do this with as many sounds as you can (whether you are inside or outside). When you can hear nothing else, listen to the silence. If you have trouble doing this, you might try pressing your index fingers tightly against your ears. After a moment or two, you will notice that the silence has a sound to it. It may sound like a bell or a thin high-pitched whine, or any number of things. Listen to whatever you hear. This is the sound of *The* creative energy. After you have practiced listening, ideas may come to you in the form of impressions. These are likely to be directions from the creative force or inner voice.

Developing Inner Sight/Tapping Into The Creative Flow

Soft Vision

Soft vision is a way of looking at things by not looking at them directly. Most of our lives we use what psychologists call "tunnel vision." Remember the saying, "You can't see the forest for the trees." It means we are looking at the trees as segments of the forest and not the forest as a whole. To the writer, soft vision is a way of seeing how details fit into the whole.

In the preceding chapter, we talked about how some people, communicating on the mental level, will see bits and pieces of things, while others, using the universal, will see things as a whole. The ones who see bits and pieces usually freeze their attention on one or another for a period of time before moving on, their minds chattering away about what their eyes are seeing. These periods of frozen attention are called tunnel vision or hard vision. Another example of hard vision is the camera. Hold a camera up to your eye and what do you see? You may see more than a tree but you still see only a small segment of the whole.

Soft vision is peripheral vision. With a little practice, we can look at something and still be aware of everything within our peripheral or entire field of vision. The physical side of this vision can be somewhat expanded but the inner side can be greatly expanded. There are exercises to help you accomplish this at the end of this chapter.

Recently I was driving down the main street of the little town of Carmel, California. There are no stop lights in Carmel and few stop signs, even though there are numerous intersections and everyone seems to move at the same time. I became very aware that I was driving with my peripheral vision, seeing the throng of vehicles going in every direction. I noticed that most other drivers were doing the same. A few frightened drivers sat dumbfounded at the intersections. They were the ones who were using hard vision. They were so frightened by the lack of traffic control and they were so focused on what individual cars were doing that they found it difficult to proceed.

When I first began to ride horseback, my instructor told me that the horse would go in the direction I looked. I was told that, if I became frightened and stared at the ground where the horse was about to step, I would make it difficult for the horse to move. My own experience with horses has taught me that this is true. I have also noticed that when I am on the trail, if I focus too hard on something just ahead, the object of my attention may frighten my horse. Most riders have had this experience at one time or another and it illustrates the expression of a "horse seeing a gremlin on the side of the trail."

Horses are noble, psychic beings. They are high-minded and are finely tuned to feelings of their rider in addition to their own inner urges. When I was a new rider, I rode my horse down the mountain on which I live and through a mile of rocky river-bed to a riding stable for riding lessons. The unevenness of the river-bed became traumatic to both me and my horse. We came to dread that part of the journey so much that it was difficult to even start down the mountain.

One day I decided to try to ride to our lesson using soft vision.

When I climbed onto my mare's back, I declared myself a vehicle for the creative force. I shifted my focus to take in my entire field of vision and then I moved the mare forward.

When we came to the bend in the road that indicated we were near the river-bed, Blossom (my horse) started to rebel. I maintained my soft vision, noticing as I did that I was without thought, and nudged Blossom forward. We continued going down the mountain. Occasionally she would stop and look back at me but, because I was not looking sharply at anything or thinking anything, her apprehension had nothing to hook itself onto and so it dissipated. We passed through the river-bed coming and going without any difficulty.

How Does Soft Vision Relate To Imagination And Daydreams?

When we are using soft vision, our attention is drawn upward between our eyes and to the center of the foreward, which is the seat of the pineal gland or what is sometimes known as the spiritual eye. This gland is engaged the moment our attention is drawn to it and peripheral vision results. When we write from this perspective, the flow of energy is not sporadic mental energy, but energy that springs from the creative force and is, therefore, unlimited.

We know from previous chapters that imagination-dreams and daydreams-is the result of images passing through the mind. Just as there can be soft and hard physical vision, there also can be soft and hard inner or imaginary vision. Remember, imaginary vision refers to the succession of images passing through the mind and is not a judgement of the images themselves. Judgement of the quality of images passing through one's mind is for the imaginer to determine.

I first discovered soft imaginary vision while writing my first book, *Through The Crystal*. As the story progressed from page to page, I realized that everything that happened was a surprise to me.

113

The characters had taken on lives of their own and I was merely writing down what I was seeing inwardly as they acted out their parts. I discovered that whenever I tried to consciously direct the scene, the flow would stop and I was dissatisfied with what came next. I found that when I mentally directed my work, I would write and rewrite and rewrite again, only to toss the results into my wastepaper basket. The creative flow would start again the moment I shifted back into soft vision.

Writing with soft vision made me aware that, as my characters spontaneously learned a lesson or discovered a profound truth, I, too, spontaneously learned and discovered. Writing then became a very exciting adventure, a tool for self-discovery.

The more I wrote, the more I yielded to this creative force, and the more I wanted to yield. I began to totally *Be* in the experiences of my characters, to live them as they lived them, feeling what they felt. As I did so, I became aware of an overlapping of consciousness in my inner and outer vision, and saw that one reflected the other. The reflection of my inner experience with my characters penetrated my outer or physical life and I became aware, really aware, of the meaning of the axiom "as above, so below."

_____

_____

_____

_____

_____

_____

_____

Writing then became a tool to effect change in my outer life. I discovered that I was each and every character in my books, the bad ones as well as the good. When there was a triumph over the negagive force in my story, I also triumphed over the negative in my outer life. The creative force had synthesized the inner and the outer. As a result, I began to develop a parallel awareness of the inner and the outer, an increased awareness in all areas of my life. I have had fewer tensions and more freedom. This method of writing works for non-fiction as well.

Tapping Into The Creative Flow

There is a certain attitude, combined with soft vision, that taps into the creative flow. The attitude is thinking *From* the end instead *Of* the end. Our imagination must see the finished product in daydreams. What we see is not a detailed account; rather, we see a peripheral completion of it.

Some Important Points

We establish patterns in all areas of our lives. Our thought patterns are reflected in all that we do, in our work and the way we react to people and situations. These thought patterns are also reflected in our writing. The patterns we use in our writing are our personal rhythms.

To communicate successfully, we must step outside our thought patterns and take a more objective approach. How do we do that? Through soft vision. From this broad field of awareness, we can write effectively in the first person, from the heart of our experience, and still be objective. We can do this in the second or third person as well but we must step outside of our thought patterns to accomplish soft vision. This is because thought patterns limit us. They blind us and make soft vision impossible. Thought patterns are made up of attitudes and these attitudes form boundaries around our consciousness.

During a crisis with Libya, the media posed the question, "How will Khadafy retaliate for our response to his assault?" The answer should not have been so difficult. The man had established reactionary patterns, which told us how he thought. His thought patterns suggested that he would try to prove his manhood through some underhanded action. It was true. The leader stationed some terrorists at major international airports and dramatized his power to the world.

Writers can create only to the extent of their consciousness. Writers, desiring to use their work as a tool for self-discovery, don't sit in front of a window looking out. They go to the other side of the window and look inward.

The unconscious state is limiting to the writer. Looking inward means to be conscious of ourselves, our feelings, our dreams, and to acknowledge what we know to ourselves. By being true to ourselves, we develop our awareness. We become aware of what is borrowed, facsimiles that are clustered around us and another's ideas that we unconsciously hold as our truths. We are then free to create from our true, personal, unlimited voice, which is found when we approach our work with soft vision.

Rhythm

A pattern is an individual's personal rhythm. When we study someone else's writing, we are observing the consciousness of that person. Through their thought patterns, we witness the individual's personal rhythm or vibrations at work in the material world. A person's thought pattern is his or her rhythm projected. This rhythm comes from the core of the individual, that which makes up the personality, and relates the consciousness with which the writer interprets life. Rhythm is the nature or consciousness of the person or thing.

People are not the only ones who have individual rhythm. Animals have it. Plants and minerals have it. Man's creations project an extension of it. A good television commercial projects the rhythmic image of its product. For example, the MacDonald's hamburger jingles make one think of hamburgers at MacDonald's. This is because some very conscious advertising executive developed the advertisment that reflects that establishment.

Just as a jingle reflects the image of an establishment, a book reflects the consciousness of its author. Writers are whatever they write or, if they write with soft vision, they become whatever they write.

Part of a writer's education is the study of the writing of other authors. By studying another's methods or patterns, we gain recognition of that writer's personal rhythm and what it says, or insight into his or her state of consciousness. This recognition can help us recognize our own personal rhythmic natures.

Children learn from adults. Until early adolescence, when they start expressing their individual natures, they parrot their parents. Again, if you want to know how the parent feels about you, pay attention to how their child responds to you. The parents may hide their feelings but the children will expose them, reflecting by facsimile what they have heard the parents say.

Rhythm shows up in a person's writing as the flow of a person's consciousness. Just as a poem has rhyme and meter, all writing and all life have rhyme and meter. The created is a reflection of the creator. Once we catch the rhythm or flow of another's writing, we come to recognize the rhythm or flow in ourselves. We learn through repetition, as a child learns from copying adults. A light bulb is turned on inside of us and shows us our own personal rhythm. Once recognized, our consciousness expands and new awarenesses advance the scale of the rhythm we possess.

Soft Sound

Rhythm reverberates to the inaudible musical vibration of the individual. As with soft and hard vision, there is also soft and hard sound. Hard sound is the physical sound around us-the song of a bird, the rush of the wind, water flowing, or the roar of a jet plane, and so on. Soft sounds are those that the physical ear doesn't hear. They are the sounds of silence and what is heard varies according to the individual's state of consciousness. Soft sounds may be similar to physical sounds: an inward tinkling of bells, the single note of a flute, or the glorious symphony of the spheres.

American Indian lore often referred to the voice within the voice of silence. Once an individual became consciously aware of this voice, his spirit was set free to soar like an eagle. Mostly it was the tribal wise men, the medicine man or shaman, who communicated these voices to the members of the tribe. For instance, the Flute Clan of the Hopis are the tribal torch bearers of the voices of the Great Silence, which is otherwise named the many voices of the Great Spirit. The creative life force is the whisperer of these voices, the source of which is God. The creative force, then, is composed of two elements - soft vision and soft sound.

More About Tapping Into The Creative Flow

When vibrations harmonize, they create a rhythm. Rhythm cannot exist without order. Organize your material. Be direct. Eliminate unnecessary words and phrases. Grasp the tools of writing by writing daily. In school we were taught to correct the incorrect. It was tedious and unbalancing to reword an unbalanced sentence. It placed us in a state of disharmony while we tried to figure it out. It felt negative. It was mechanical. Creative writing is not mechanical. Through the use of patterns and by rewriting the harmonious work of authors we admire, we can capture the essence of creativity. For example, spelling is most successfully taught by phonetics, not memorization. Teaching phonetics is really teaching the rhythm or sound of a word and how to interpret the letters that form a word. Learning to write creatively is catching the rhythm or flow of your individual self. Creative writing, like spirituality, is something that cannot be taught but must be caught.

E X E R C I S E   12

Developing Soft Vision: Paper Technique

Draw a circle about the size of a dime in the center of an eight-and-a-half by eleven inch sheet of paper. In each of the four corners, draw an X approximately two inches high. Now, hold the paper horizontally up to your face so that your nose touches the circle in the center of the page. Look straight ahead and focus your attention on the paper directly in front of your eyes. The paper will be so close that it will not be easy to do but try anyway. Next, slowly count to thirty, allowing yourself to relax your gaze a bit more with each count. Notice that your focus is becoming diffused and that your field of vision is gradually expanding.

1. You should be able to see the edge of the paper clearly to the left and right sides. What do you see beyond the edges? (Suppose you see books in a bookcase to your right. Can you determine the color of any of the books? Can you see a nicknack on any of the shelves?)

2. Without focusing your vision, can you see the X in each of the four corners of the paper? One corner? Two corners? Three corners? It may take a moment before you can see them and you may not see them all. Can you see beyond any of those corners? What do you see?

3. Fold back the four corners of the paper so that the X's are no longer visible (see diagram). Now hold the paper up to your face again. What do you see beyond the edges of the paper?

Do this exercise once or twice a day for a week, or until you can see beyond the edges of the paper. Make notes about what you see, including items, sizes, shapes, and colors. For variety, try the exercise in different rooms in your house and even outdoors. You will be amazed at what you see and how developed your peripheral vision becomes after a few short exercises.

EXERCISE 13

Developing Peripheral Senses: Walking Technique

Plan to go for a walk along a quiet street, in a meadow, a park or any other place you feel comfortable alone. Before you set out, place a two-inch piece of cellophane tape between your eyes, in the center of your forehead. The tape should be placed vertically. Only the top half-inch nearest your hairline should be fastened tightly. The lower half, near the eyes, should hang loose, sticking out so that you can see it.

Take a deep breath and relax. Allow your arms to swing freely at your sides with the fingers of your hands curled slightly inward. Keep your eyes focused on the piece of tape and begin walking.

Most probably you won't really see the tape but only a filmy image of it. This is fine because you are not really interested in the tape itself, only in the point of focus that it gives you. Your vision will be diffused and this is what we want. You will notice that you can see everything indirectly from the outside corner of your left eye to the outside corner of your right eye, up to the sky, and down to the ground. This is the field of your peripheral vision.

Pause and make a mental note of what you can see in this way. Now continue to walk again, noting how the depth of your perception changes as you move. As you move forward, you perceive new sights and those behind you recede and disappear. Things that were small are larger and things that were large become small and disappear. Walking in this way, you may get the feeling that your body is a vehicle like any other vehicle and you are inside of it looking out.

Keep your attention on the piece of cellophane tape and continue to walk.

1.   What do you see? Without straining, try to see what is beyond your right shoulder. What do you perceive near and far. Now look beyond your left shoulder. Again, what do you perceive

near and far?

2. Listen as you walk. Note the sounds you hear. Is there an overall sound to the place where you are walking? Are there certain distinct sounds? Can you identify them? Try standing still for a moment and close your eyes. Listen for the overall sound; for individual sounds. Is there a feeling to the area? Open your eyes again and continue to walk and listen with your peripheral senses.

When you return home, take a few moments to note your impressions in your journal. Do this every day for a week, if you can. At the end of that time, you should make some interesting discoveries.

Writing From Your Peripheral Senses

Work with the other exercises in this book before trying this one. It may even be helpful to review all of the earlier exercises to get the principles we are working with clearly in your mind.

Decide what it is that you want to write - a novel, short story, magazine article, essay, office memo, or letter. Sit down in front of your computer or your typewriter or with pen in hand. Close your eyes and take a few deep breaths. Now, with your eyes closed, imagine that you are looking at the piece of cellophane tape in the center of your forehead. Look and then listen in an unfocused way, declaring yourself an open vehicle for the creative force. When you feel relaxed and the piece of cellophane tape image is clearly in your mind, open your eyes again and begin writing.

Don't think about what you will write. You want to write from the impressions of your peripheral senses and that means that the words will come to you subtly, in bits and pieces. As you sit poised and ready to begin, a few words will come to you. Don't worry about what will follow once it is written down, just write and what follows will follow.

The more you practice this technique, the more proficient you will become at it. This approach to writing is not new. To the writer, it is the key to discovering one's self through one's art.

Conclusion

Life is the result of a succession of images passing through our minds. Everytime we align our actions with our dreams, life becomes everything we daydream it to be.

* * *

As these images passed from my mind onto the paper, it occurred to me that the writing of this book could be defined as a waking dream, and that, you, the reader were sharing the dream with me. It also occurred to me that the dream, writing or reading, was merely a tool to promote some end. Both can be tools for self-discovery. All things, all places, and all events can be tools for self-discovery.

Heather Hughes-Calero's books are available at your book store or direct from your publisher.

- -

Order Form

Please send me the following books by Heather Hughes-Calero:

No. of Copies	Title	Price	Amt.
_____	**WRITING AS A TOOL FOR SELF-DISCOVERY**	$8.95	_____
_____	**THE GOLDEN DREAM** (Hard Cover)	12.95	_____
	THE SEDONA TRILOGY (paperback)		
_____	Book 1: **THROUGH THE CRYSTAL**	7.95	_____
_____	Book 2: **DOORWAY BETWEEN THE WORLDS**	7.95	_____
_____	Book 3: **LAND OF NOME**	7.95	_____
		TOTAL	$ _____

Shipping:
(1 to 3 books $1.00, 50¢ per book additional)   _____

California Residents add 6% sales tax.   _____

U.S.A. FUNDS ONLY
TOTAL ENCLOSED
(check or money order) $ _____

Please print

NAME _____

ADDRESS_____

CITY _____ STATE _____ ZIP _____

- -

Coastline Publishing Company
P.O. Box 223062
Carmel, California 93922
(408) 625-9388